Let's get Cooking!

Printed and bound in the UK by
Severn, Bristol Road, Gloucester, GL2 5EU

ISBN: 978-1-912535-58-3

Published by
Candy Jar Books
Mackintosh House
136 Newport Road, Cardiff, CF24 1DJ
www.candyjarbooks.co.uk

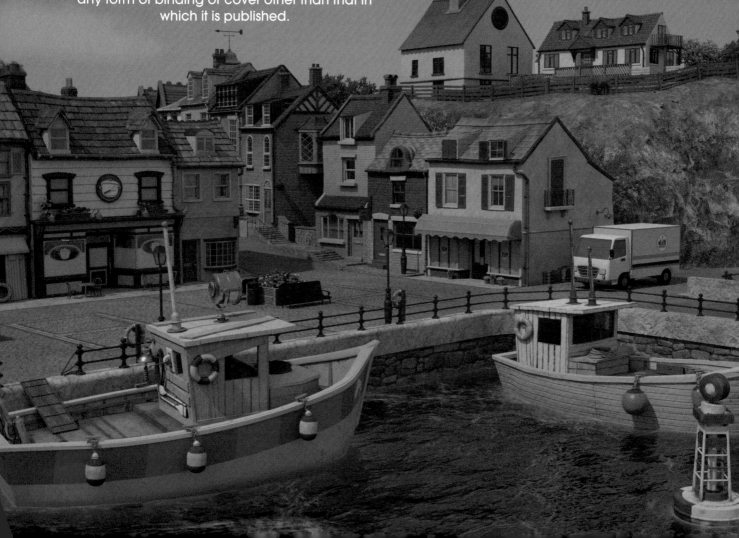

Shane the Chef

This Book Belongs to:

_____

_____

_____

Sizzling Saucepans!

It's my first cookbook! Now you can enjoy trying out some of the recipes from my TV show. I've selected a mix of quick and easy healthy meals and of course a few treats. So get your aprons on and Let's Get Cooking!

Shane

Contents

With Thanks

Hoho Entertainment would like to thank everyone that has been involved in helping Shane the Chef publish his first cookbook. In particular, we'd like to thank the BDA (British Dietetic Association) for their guidance on all the recipes.

"It's been a privilege for the BDA to be involved in both the Shane the Chef *TV series and now this cookbook. We hope it becomes the go-to manual for kids and their parents and carers to create tasty healthy meals together at home."*
Doctor Frankie Phillips, RD.

The Association of UK Dietitians

Also a huge thank you from Shane to the following people for trying out his recipes:

Robbie Stringer, Jenny Litchfield,
Lottie James, Louise Kelly,
Justin Wilkes, Anna-Lisa Jenaer,
Oliver Ellis, Helen Howells,
Will Rees, Keren Williams,
Shaun Russell.

Are You Ready to Cook?

My daughter Izzy loves to help me in the kitchen, but it's important to always have a grown-up with you to make sure that you stay safe while having fun cooking up my recipes.

So before you get started, let me give you a few tips:

Ingredients – make sure you have all the ingredients and utensils you'll need before you start cooking.

Weights and Measuring – to keep things simple, we're using metric (grams and millilitres) in this book.

Tablespoons (tbsps.) and Teaspoons (tsps.) – to be accurate, it's best to use measuring spoons but you can use normal spoons too. Be careful not to mix them up.

Clean hands – before you start cooking, always wash your hands first. If you are preparing raw meat or fish, be sure to wash your hands and any knives and chopping boards as soon as you've finished and before doing the rest of your food preparation.

Put on your apron – things can get a little messy so pop on your apron before you get started.

Oven Gloves – make sure your grown-up is wearing oven gloves when they take the hot food out of the oven for you.

Salt – you'll notice that we don't use salt for seasoning in these recipes. Instead we suggest other ways to season your food such as using freshly ground pepper and other herbs and spices.

Let's get Cooking!

Eggs Anywhichway

Cracking!

Try boiled and scrambled eggs as well!

"Watch me make them in Episode 1 Eggs Anywhichway"

Frying Pan

Whisk

Spatula

What you will need

Omelette
Serves 1
Prep and cook time: 10 mins

2 eggs
Freshly ground black pepper
1 tsp. olive or vegetable oil
40-50g desired fillings
(cheese, ham, cooked
mushrooms for example)

Fried Eggs
Serves 1
Prep and cook time: 5 mins

2 eggs
1 tsp. olive or vegetable oil
Freshly ground black pepper

Omelette

1 Beat the eggs and ground pepper together in a bowl.

2 Heat the oil in a frying pan over a medium heat until sizzling, ensuring the oil coats the bottom of the pan.

3 Add the beaten eggs (you can tell if the pan is hot enough as the mixture should set at the edges as soon as it is added).

5 Once the top of the liquid egg mixture is almost cooked, add the fillings to one side of omlette. Fold the other half over. Cook for a further 30 seconds.

Fried Eggs

1 Heat the oil over a medium heat in a non-stick frying pan.

2 Crack the eggs into the frying pan and fry until the egg turns white.

3 Serve on their own or on toast, with a sprinkling of freshly ground black pepper (or as part of a hearty breakfast).

4 Using the spatula push the liquid egg mixture towards the centre, so that all the liquid eggs are cooked.

Shane's top tip:

To make your omlette a little creamier, add a splodge of Greek yoghurt or crème fraîche to the egg mixture.

Tomato Soup

Soup-erb!

Serve with crusty bread!

"Watch me and Dad make it in Episode 3 Who's Cooking?"

Bowl

What you will need

Serves 4
Prep and cook time: 50 mins

3 tbsps. olive oil
1 medium onion
10 large tomatoes
2 tbsps. tomato purée (2 squirts)
350ml vegetable stock
1 heaped tbsp. thyme, chopped
Freshly ground black pepper

Knife

Wooden Spoon

Saucepan

1 Finely chop the onion and then chop the tomatoes into small chunks.

2 Heat the oil over a medium heat in a large saucepan. Add the onions and gently cook or 'sweat' for about 7 mins, without letting the onions brown.

3 Add the chopped tomatoes, stock, tomato purée, thyme and some freshly ground pepper to the pan. Simmer for 30-40 mins.

4 Blend everything in a blender and return to the pan. Simmer for a further 5 mins.

5 Serve. Add steamed peas if you like.

Shane's top tip:

You can also add a blob of natural yoghurt or crème fraîche in the middle of each bowl and swirl with a spoon.

Baked Potatoes

Spud-tacular!

Try wih cream cheese as well!

"Watch me make them in Episode 38 Potato Day"

Baking Tray

Spoon   Knife

Bowl

What you will need

Serves 4
Prep and cook time: 30-60 mins depending on method used

Baked Potato
4 large potatoes
Olive oil

1. Tuna
2 x 146g tins of tuna
(drain off oil or spring water)
4 tbsps. mayonnaise
1 x 165g tin of sweetcorn

2. Cheese and Beans
1 can of baked beans
Grated hard cheese (as much as you like). Cheddar is good!

3. Prawns
125g cooked prawns
½ lemon
2 tsps. tomato purée
3 tbsps. crème fraîche

Potatoes

1

Prick the potatoes with a fork. Rub with olive oil. Wrap in tin foil.

2

Put the potatoes onto an oven tray.

3

Bake at 200°C / Gas mark 6 for 45-60 mins.

4

Peel back the tin foil and test with a sharp knife. If it slides into the potato easily, then it's done.

Cheese and Beans

Heat the beans in a saucepan on a medium heat. Pour over a quartered potato. Grate cheese on top and serve.

Tuna and Sweetcorn

Drain the tuna and place in a bowl with the sweetcorn. Add the mayonnaise and mix thoroughly. Spoon over potato.

Prawn Cocktail

Place the crème fraîche and tomato purée in a bowl and mix until it turns pink. Squeeze the lemon juice into the bowl. Add the prawns and mix thoroughly.

5

Make a cross in the potato and open up by pressing each side with fingers and thumbs. Drizzle with a little olive oil, then add your chosen filling.

Shane's time saving tip:

Once you have pricked the potatoes with a fork and rubbed with olive oil, place them in a heatproof dish. Cover with cling film, place in the microwave and cook on full power for between 12-15 mins (less time for less potatoes). When you can slide a knife easily into all the potatoes, remove them from the microwave, wrap in foil then place onto a baking tray and finish off in the oven for around 10-15 mins to get a lovely golden and slightly crisp potato skin.

Tricolore Salad

Healthy!

Eat with some nice wholemeal bread!

"Watch me make it in Episode 2 Pig on the Loose"

What you will need

Knife

Plate

Serves 4
Prep time: 10-15 mins

4 large tomatoes
2 avocados
2 x 125g packs of mozzarella
Extra virgin olive oil
Balsamic vinegar
Freshly ground black pepper

1

Slice the tomatoes
and the mozzarella.

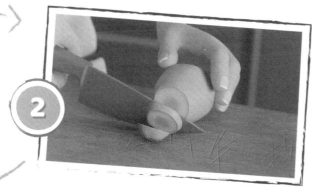

2

Cut the avocados in half and
remove the stones, then slice.

3

Arrange the salad by layering the
tomatoes, avocado and mozzarella
in a circle.

4

Finish with a drizzle of olive oil,
balsamic vinegar and some
freshly ground black pepper.

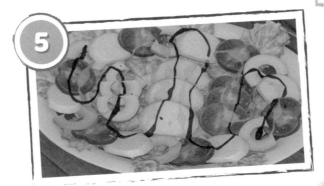

5

Serve.

Shane's top tip:

Each time you make my salad, get a little more
adventurous and try adding some new ingredients
e.g. black olives, lettuce, cucumber, etc.

Portrait Pizza

Pizza-licious!

"Watch me make it in Episode 10 Master Pizza"

Get creative with your own pizza making!

Saucepan

Bowl

Rolling Pin

What you will need

Makes 1 large deep crust pizza or 2 thin crust pizzas
Prep and cook time: 50-60 mins
(the dough needs to rise)

For the Dough

375g plain flour
1 tsp. salt
1 tsp. dried active baking yeast
2 tbsps. olive oil
225ml warm water (45°C)

For the Tomato Sauce

1 clove of garlic, crushed
15g basil, chopped
2 tbsps. olive oil
8 fresh tomatoes
(chopped or a carton of plain tomato passata)
Freshly ground black pepper

For the Topping:
Grated mozzarella

1

Mix the flour, salt and yeast in a bowl.

2

Gradually add the olive oil and water. Mix together until it forms a dough ball.

3

Knead the dough ball on a lightly floured surface for a minute or two. Really use your strength!

4

Using your hands, flatten the ball into a circle and roll it out to make a pizza base shape. Place a clean tea towel over the top for around 30 mins (divide dough into two if making thin crust pizza).

7

Smear the cooled tomato sauce over the pizza dough base and add desired toppings

6

Turn down to a low heat. Add the chopped tomatoes or passata, basil and some freshly ground black pepper. Simmer for 20 mins to thicken sauce.

5

Meanwhile, for the sauce, heat the olive oil over a medium heat in a non-stick pan. Add the garlic and stir.

8

Bake at 190°C / Gas mark 5 for 15-20 mins until the dough edges have browned.

Shane's top tip:

Why not try making a portrait pizza like we did using different ingredients such as sliced pepperoni, shredded chicken, cooked sliced ham, mushrooms or diced pineapple?

Fish Wraps
with Peach Salsa

Tangy!

"Watch Shane make these in Episode 12 Dancing Under the Stars"

Tastes great with rice, tomato and bean salad!

What you will need

Serves 4
Prep and cook time: 20-30 mins

2 ripe peaches, peeled and diced
1 red pepper, finely chopped
1 red onion, finely chopped
2-3 tbsps. olive oil
½ lime, freshly squeezed
4 fillets of white fish
4 tortilla wraps

Bowl

Wooden Spoon

Oven Glove

Baking Tray

Knife

Place the peach, pepper, onion and coriander in a large bowl. Add 1 tbsp. olive oil and the lime juice, then mix together.

Season to taste with pepper. Cover and refrigerate until ready to use.

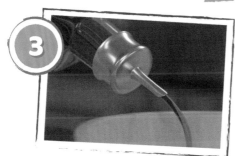

Brush fish with olive oil and place under a grill on a medium heat.

Cook for 2-3 minutes on each side until done.

Warm the tortillas in a frying pan on a low heat. Stack on a plate and cover with tin foil to keep warm until you're ready to fill.

Place a tortilla on a plate. Add a fish fillet with a large spoonful of salsa on the top. Wrap or roll the tortilla around the filling and serve.

Shane's top tip:

Choose pollock if you want sustainable fish. Go for wholemeal tortilla wraps for a healthier choice.

Cauliflower Rice & Chicken Curry

Spicy!

Tastes great with naan or wholemeal chapati and chutney!

"Watch me make this dish in Episode 25 Mama Polenta's Date Night"

What you will need

Serves 4
Prep and cook time: 30-40 mins

1 large cauliflower
4 boneless chicken breasts
1 tbsp. turmeric
1 tbsp. garam masala
½ tbsp. ground ginger
1 green pepper, chopped
1 large onion, finely chopped
2 tomatoes, chopped
2 cloves garlic, crushed
2 tbsps. coriander, chopped
Freshly ground black pepper
Cup of water (100ml)
Vegetable or sunflower oil
4 chapatis

Oven Glove

Wooden Spoon

Bowl

Frying Pan

Saucepan

Cauliflower

1

Grate the cauliflower using the coarse side of the grater (or whizz in a food processor using the small blade setting).

2

Sautée in a pan over a medium heat with 1 tsp. oil, cover with lid and cook in the frying pan for 5-8 minutes, or...

3

Bake in the oven. Spread the grated cauliflower in a thin even layer onto a baking tray. Drizzle with olive oil and bake at 200°C / Gas mark 6 for 12 mins, stirring halfway through.

Curry

1

Cut the chicken into small chunks and place in a mixing bowl.

2

Add turmeric, garam masala and ginger. Make sure chicken is coated, then set aside.

3

Heat oil in the saucepan over a medium heat. Add the onion and garlic and fry until golden brown. Then add the chicken and cook for 5 mins.

4

Add the green pepper and tomotoes, water and black pepper. Bring to the boil and simmer for 20 mins or until the sauce has thickened.

5

Sprinkle with coriander and serve with cauliflower rice and a warm chapati.

Shane's top tip:

To make the curry a little creamier, add a splodge of Greek yoghurt or crème fraîche and stir it in before sprinkling on the coriander. For a meat free alternative, simply replace chicken with vegetables, such as butternut squash, sweet potato or spinach.

Butternut Squash Fritters

"Watch me make them in Episode 19 Pony Problem"

Delicious!

These fritters are just perfect with a salad!

What you will need

Makes 8 Fritters
Prep and cook time: 15 mins

550g butternut squash
150g wholemeal flour
1 large egg, beaten
Freshly ground black pepper
1 small onion, finely chopped
1 tbsp. fresh sage
Vegetable oil

Knife

Sieve

Masher

Wooden Spoon

Frying Pan

Saucepan

1 Peel and chop the butternut squash into chunks. Place in a saucepan of cold water, bring to the boil and simmer until soft.

2 Drain the butternut squash, place in a large bowl and mash it.

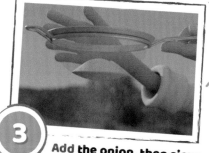

3 Add the onion, then sieve the flour into the bowl.

4 Finely chop the sage and add to the mixture.

5 Season with a little freshly ground pepper.

6 Slowly add the beaten egg and mix to bind, making sure the mixture doesn't get too wet.

7 Separate the mixture into 8 equal sections. Using clean hands, take a section of mixture, roll into a ball then flatten to make a fritter.

8 Heat oil in a large frying pan or griddle on a medium heat and cook the fritters for 2-3 mins on each side until golden brown.

Shane's top tip:

For potato and courgette fritters, grate 2 potatoes and 1 courgette. Squeeze out any excess water, then add onion, flour and seasoning. Mix 1 egg in a jug and slowly add to the mixing bowl. Don't let the mixture get too runny. Heat oil in a large frying pan and drop in spoonfuls of the mixture. Fry for 2-3 minutes on each side until golden.

Pak Choi Stir Fry

Tasty!

Serve with wholewheat noodles!

"Watch me make it in Episode 33 Food Festival"

What you will need

Serves 4
Prep and cook time: 15 mins

1 tbsp. olive oil
1 thumb-sized piece of ginger, grated
1 clove of garlic, crushed
4 spring onions, finely chopped
1 red pepper, thinly sliced
8 baby pak choi, leaves separated
Freshly ground black pepper
Wholewheat noodles
(approx. 50g per serving)

Knife

Spatula

Frying Pan

Heat the oil in a frying pan or wok over a medium heat for 1-2 mins.

Add the garlic and grated ginger, then heat until lightly coloured.

Stir in the peppers, spring onions and pak choi and turn up the heat a little.

Cook and stir for 5-8 mins until the pak choi turns bright green.

Add some freshly ground black pepper. Serve with wholewheat noodles.

Shane's top tip:

For fussy eaters, start by using vegetables you know they like (yellow peppers, mushrooms, broccoli, soya beans, etc), then introduce new and different types of vegetables like pak choi.

Aubergine Parmigiana

"Watch Shane make it in Episode 39 Recipe for Disaster"

Delizioso!

Mama Polenta's special winter warmer!

What you will need

Serves 4-6
Prep and cook time: 60 mins

4 large aubergines
1 x 500g carton tomato passata
1 tbsp. tomato purée
Splash of Worcester sauce
2 tbsps. grated Parmesan or hard cheese
2 tbsps. breadcrumbs
2 tbsps. olive oil

Dish

Knife

Oven Glove

Saucepan

Baking Tray

1

Preheat oven to
180°C / Gas mark 5.

2

Slice the aubergines into circles
5-10mm thick and place on a
non-stick baking tray (you
may need a few trays).

3

Brush with the olive oil and
cook in the oven for 20 mins,
turning halfway through.

4

Warm the passata gently in a pan,
adding the tomato purée and Worcester
sauce. Allow to thicken a little.

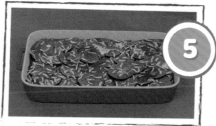

5

Using a deep ovenproof dish (approx. 24cm x 24cm),
place a layer of cooked aubergine on the bottom,
sprinkle a layer of mozzarella and then cover
with several spoonfuls of tomato sauce. Repeat
the process until you have 3-4 layers.

6

On the last layer, sprinkle the breadcrumbs
and Parmesan cheese over the top of the
tomato sauce.

7

Bake for 25-30 mins until the
top is golden brown.

Shane's top tip:

For a heartier option, gently brown 400g
of boneless chicken thighs in a large frying pan.
Place the chicken in the bottom of the oven dish,
layer with one or two layers of aubergine, sprinkle
with mozzarella and top with tomato sauce, Parmesan
and breadcrumbs. Bake for 30-35 mins at 180°C / Gas mark 5.

Fancy Fish Fingers

Always a favourite!

Tastes great in a sandwich!

"Watch Shane make them in Episode 18 Fancy Fish Fingers"

What you will need

Serves 4 (makes approximately 8 fish fingers)
Prep and cook time: 20-25 mins

30g cornflakes
200g fillet of sustainable white fish (pollock is a good choice)
20g plain flour
1 egg
Freshly ground black pepper

Baking Tray

Bowl

Whisk

Oven Glove

Rolling Pin

Preheat oven to 200°C / Gas mark 6 and cover the baking tray with greaseproof paper.

Place the flour into a mixing bowl and season with a little freshly ground black pepper.

Break an egg into a separate bowl and beat with a fork or whisk.

Place the cornflakes in another bowl and crush with the end of a rolling pin.

Slice the fish into strips, dip into the flour mix, then into the beaten egg and then into the cornflakes.

Place on a baking tray and bake for 12-14 mins or until done. Remember to turn the fish fingers halfway through cooking.

Shane's top tip:

To ensure fish is cooked through, always do the flaky test. Carefully use a fork or toothpick to prise a section of the fish apart. If it flakes away, they are ready to eat!

Lamb Kebabs

Mmmmmm!

Serve with rice and salad!

"Watch me make them in Episode 44 No Go Kart"

What you will need

Knife

Bowl

Skewer

Serves 4
Prep and cook time: 20 mins

Marinade

4 tbsps. olive oil
2 tbsps. soy sauce
3 tbsps. red wine vinegar
1 tbsp. honey
2 cloves garlic, crushed
Freshly ground black pepper

Kebab

4 medium-sized lamb fillets, cut into 3cm chunks
1 large yellow pepper
1 courgette
1-2 medium red onions
4 medium tomatoes
8 wooden skewers

1 Mix all the marinade ingredients together in a bowl and then add the lamb chunks and mix well. Cover and leave in the fridge for an hour.

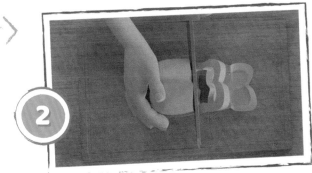

2 Chop the vegetables into chunks about the same size as the meat.

3 Thread the meat and vegetables onto the skewers.

4 Brush the kebabs with any remaining marinade and place under the grill.

5 Grill on a high heat for 8-10 mins, turning occasionally.

6 Let the kebabs rest for 5 mins before serving.

Shane's top tip:

Soak the skewers in water for at least 30 mins before grilling as this will stop them burning on the grill.

Mouth-watering!

Broad Bean Risotto

"Watch me make it in Episode 40 Truffle Kerfuffle"

Swap broad beans for soya beans!

What you will need

Serves 4-6
Prep and cook time: 30 mins

1 tbsp. olive oil
320g Arborio/risotto rice
1.5 litres hot vegetable stock
1 white onion, finely chopped
1 cup of broad beans (if frozen soak in hot water for a few mins)
1 tbsp. finely grated truffle (optional)
2 tbsps. crème fraîche or plain Greek yoghurt
2 tbsps. finely grated Parmesan

Wooden Spoon

Ladle

Heavy-bottomed Frying Pan

Heat the oil in a large heavy-bottomed saucepan or frying pan on a medium to high heat.

Add the onion and soften without letting it burn / brown.

Add the rice and stir with a wooden spoon, making sure the rice is coated with onions and oil.

Add 1 to 1½ ladles of stock and stir. Allow to simmer and absorb, then add another ladle (being careful not to let the rice stick to the bottom of the pan). DON'T leave the pan unattended. Stir every few minutes.

After 15-20 mins the rice should be softening. Add the broad beans and continue to cook, adding stock as before until the stock has been absorbed but the risotto is still moist.

Remove from the heat and stir in 1 tbsp. of grated Parmesan. Then stir in the crème fraîche or Greek yoghurt.

Sprinkle with Parmesan cheese and a little grated truffle (optional) and allow to rest for a few minutes before serving.

Shane's top tip:

For a change swap broad beans for soya beans. Or why not try chicken, broccoli and pea risotto? Lightly steam broccoli and peas. About 15 mins into cooking, add the rice, cooked chicken and vegetables. Continue cooking until the rice is soft. Finish with Greek yoghurt or crème fraîche and Parmesan. Fussy eater? Then start with a simple ham and pea risotto.

Mushroom Burgers

"Watch me make them in Episode 30 Brilliant Burgers"

Banging!

A healthy alternative to beef burgers!

What you will need

Serves 4
Prep and cook time: 30-40 mins

250g mushrooms
1 medium onion, very finely chopped
60g dried breadcrumbs
30g of plain flour
2 tbsps. dried oregano
A handful of parsley, finely chopped
Freshly ground black pepper
3 medium large eggs, beaten
Vegetable or sunflower oil
Burger buns (wholemeal is best)

Wooden Spoon

Bowl

Frying Pan

1

Chop the mushrooms into small pieces and place in a large mixing bowl. Add the onion, breadcrumbs, flour, oregano, parsley and black pepper. Mix thoroughly.

2

Slowly add the beaten egg until the mixture can be moulded but isn't too wet (you may not need all the egg).

3

Separate the mixture into 4 or 6 sections, then using clean hands, mould each one into 4 thick (or 6 smaller) burger-shaped patties.

4

Heat some oil in a frying pan over a medium heat and add the burgers or place under the grill. Cook for 3-4 mins on each side making sure they are cooked through.

5

Serve in a burger bun with lettuce, sliced tomato and a sauce of your choice (e.g. mayonnaise or ketchup).

Shane's top tip:

Why not make some sweet potato chips to go with it, like I did in Episode 5, "Easy Cheesy"? Simply cut sweet potatoes into strips, place on a baking tray, drizzle with olive oil and bake at 180°C / Gas mark 5 for 20-25 mins, turning halfway through.

Spinach Meatballs

"Watch Shane make them in Episode 17 Where's Eddy"

Result!

A classic dish with a green twist!

Frying Pan

Saucepan

Bowl

Whisk

What you will need

Serves 4
Prep and cook time: 40 mins

Meatballs

500g minced beef
280g spinach, chopped
½ onion, finely chopped
1 clove of garlic, crushed
¼ tsp. dried oregano
120g wholemeal breadcrumbs
Freshly ground black pepper
1 large egg, beaten

Tomato Sauce

2 tsps. olive oil
4 cloves of garlic, crushed
2 x 400g tin of chopped tomatoes
1 onion, finely chopped
Freshly ground black pepper

1 Place the minced beef in a large mixing bowl.

2 Add the spinach and the rest of the meatball ingredients (except the egg) and mix with a wooden spoon.

3 Slowly add the beaten egg, until the mixture can be moulded but isn't too wet (you may not need all the egg).

4 Using clean hands take a small bit of the mixture and roll between both hands to make a ball. Continue this until all the mixture is finished. Pop meatballs in the fridge to firm while preparing the sauce.

5 In a large saucepan, heat the olive oil on a low medium heat. Once hot, add the garlic. When the garlic is golden brown, add the tomatoes, onion and pepper. Cover with lid, reduce heat and simmer for 10 mins.

6 In a large non-stick frying pan, add 1 tbsp. of olive oil on a medium heat. Once oil is hot, add as many meatballs as you can fit. Cook, turning the meatballs often, until all sides are browned.

7 When cooked through, drain excess oil and drop the meatballs into tomato sauce. Put back on a low heat and simmer for an additional 15-20 minutes. Serve with wholewheat spaghetti.

Shane's top tip:

If you like a zing, then add a little chilli powder or paprika to the tomato sauce – and don't forget to sprinkle on some grated Parmesan cheese for the perfect finish!

Beetroot Cupcakes

Yummy!

"Watch me make them in Episode 22 In the Pink"

These cupcakes are perfect for picnics or as an afternoon snack!

What you will need

Makes 12 Cupcakes
Prep and cook time: 30 mins

150g self-raising flour
1 tsp. baking powder
1 - 1½ tbsp. cocoa powder
50g light soft brown sugar
100g cooked beetroot
1 egg
125ml semi-skimmed milk
50ml vegetable oil

Sieve

Bowl

Wooden Spoon

Oven Glove

Whisk

Knife

1 Preheat the oven to 180°C / Gas mark 4.

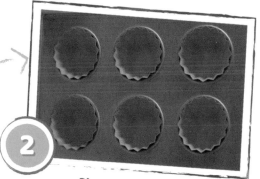

2 Place the cupcake cases in a cupcake baking tray.

3 Sieve the flour, baking powder and cocoa powder into a large mixing bowl. Add the sugar.

4 Put the beetroot, egg, milk and oil into a blender and whizz until smooth.

5 Pour the liquid into the dry ingredients and mix until thoroughly combined. Do not over mix.

6 Spoon into cupcake cases, leaving room for the mixture to rise.

7 Bake in the oven for about 15 mins or until the cakes have risen and are springy when pressed.

8 Cool in the cases on a wire cooling rack.

Shane's top tip:

Why not pop a blob of Greek yoghurt or crème fraîche on top? Try mixing with some beetroot juice to give your topping some added colour.

Baked Apples

Tasty!

Lovely with a dollop of Greek yoghurt or crème fraîche!

"Watch me make them in Episode 16 Izzy in Charge"

What you will need

Serves 4
Prep and cook time: 60 mins

4 large baking / eating apples
4 tbsps. honey
25g melted butter
1 tbsp. cinnamon
40g chopped almonds (optional)
40g currants / chopped raisins
¼ cup boiling water

Baking Tray

Bowl

Wooden Spoon

Knife

1 Preheat the oven to 190°C / Gas mark 5.

2 Mix the honey, butter, cinnamon, chopped almonds and raisins in a bowl and set aside.

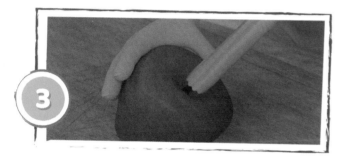

3 Core the apples (using either an apple corer or a sharp knife) leaving 1 cm of apple at the bottom. Cut a tiny slice off the bottom if they don't stand up on the tray.

4 Score a line around the middle circumference of the apples. This helps to stop them bursting.

5 Put the apples on a baking tray and stuff with the honey, dried fruit and nut mix.

6 Pour the boiling water into the bottom of the baking dish and bake for 30-45 minutes, until cooked through and tender, but not overdone and mushy.

Shane's top tip:

Once baked, use the juices from the bottom of the tray and drizzle over the apples.

Pancakes

Lovely!

Serve with fruit, berries, crème fraîche or frozen yoghurt!

"Watch Shane make them in Episode 28 Going Bananas"

What you will need

Serves 4
Prep and cook time: 30 mins

140g plain flour
1 tsp. baking powder
½ tsp salt
1 egg, beaten
225ml milk
50ml sunflower or vegetable oil
2 medium bananas
Lemon juice

Whisk

Knife

Wooden Spoon

Bowl

Frying Pan

1 Sift the flour and baking powder into a large bowl and stir through. Add the salt and stir through.

2 Add the egg and milk and beat well.

3 Heat a little oil in a non-stick frying pan on a medium heat

4 Pour half a ladle of the pancake batter into the pan and cook for 1-2 minutes, flipping when the edges look cooked and the bubbles on the surface begin to break.

5 Chop up some bananas, place in a line down the middle of the pancake. Wrap the pancake around the filling, drizzle with lemon juice and serve.

Shane's top tip:

If you don't like bananas, then try filling with other fruits or berries and serve with crème fraîche or frozen yoghurt.

Rice Pudding

Scrumptious!

A comforting pudding on a cold winter's day!

"Watch me make this in Episode 45 Peekamoo!"

What you will need

Serves 4
Prep and cook time: 2 ½ hours

2 pints full fat milk
140g pudding or Arborio rice
60g caster sugar
Nutmeg to sprinkle
Butter to grease the oven dish

Oven Glove

Wooden Spoon

Bowl

Dish

Saucepan

1

Preheat the oven to 140°C / Gas mark 2.

2

Grease a large ovenproof dish with butter.

3

Bring the milk to a simmer in a saucepan.

4

Add the rice and sugar to the milk and stir.

5

Pour the mixture into the ovenproof dish.

6

Sprinkle with nutmeg.

7

Bake for 2 hours, stirring the pudding halfway through.

Shane's top tip:

Why not use some chopped dried apricots, dried berries or sultanas instead of sugar?

Cherry Crumble

"Watch my dad make this great pudding in Episode 41 Cherry Tree Rescue"

Delicious!

Serve with custard, crème fraîche or frozen yoghurt!

What you will need

Serves 4/6
Prep and cook time: 45 mins

800g cherries, pitted and halved
2 tbsp. natural golden caster sugar
2 tbsp. water
75g wholemeal flour
50g porridge oats
50g unsalted butter (softened)
100g chopped almonds
50g demerara sugar

Oven Glove

Wooden Spoon

Bowl

Ovenproof Dish

1 Preheat the oven to 190°C / Gas mark 5.

2 Using a little butter, grease the bottom of a deep-sided overproof dish (approx 24cm x 20cm).

3 Place the cherries and water in a saucepan and cook on a low heat for 6-8 mins. Add the caster sugar and simmer for a further 5 mins or until soft. Set aside to cool.

4 In a mixing bowl, use your fingertips to rub the butter into the flour until it forms fine crumbs.

5 Add the oats, brown sugar and almonds, and stir to form a crumbly mixture.

6 Transfer the cherries into the ovenproof dish, then sprinkle the crumble on top of the fruit and bake in the oven for 25-30 mins or until the crumble turns golden brown.

Shane's top tip:

If you've got a fussy eater that doesn't like cherries, then try spiced apple crumble. Simply peel and slice 8-10 apples. Place on a roasting tray, sprinkle over 2 tbsp. of light brown soft sugar, add ½ tsp. cinnamon and ½ tsp. all spice and ½ cup of apple or orange juice. Bake in the oven at 180°C / Gas mark 4 for around 20 mins. Leave the fruit to cool, then transfer to the baking dish and follow the remaining steps as above.